"Quote Therapy"
Session 1

SABRENA S. HENDERSON

ISBN: 0-692-67316-4
ISBN-13: 978-0-692-67316-4

DEDICATION

There isn't a single struggle that could break me, and I developed the skill of overcoming. So I dedicate this book to the struggle itself and anybody in it.
Stand tall and walk confidently through your struggles. You're going to come out stronger if you don't break.
Keep in mind, For The Beauty of it All…

ACKNOWLEDGMENTS

This book is directly inspired by the responses to #MotivationalMonday of Y.M.E

SESSION 1

"Running from pain can be more damaging then the pain itself. Pain is sometimes the gateway to freedom..."

- Running prevents you from acknowledging problems and issues at hand.

- Sweeping issues under the rug is a common way of running, and it will cause the issue/problem to pile up and fester.

- Write the specific issue down, then write how it makes you feel and why it makes you run.

- Then you can begin to figure out why you're running in the first place. Is it fear? Is it insecurities? Is it pride?

"Having CHANGED and

having GROWN

can easily be mistaken

one for the other..."

- Changing is becoming someone else other than your true self.

- Change should only be necessary to personal preferences.

- Change and growth are similar in the fact that they both bring about a difference, but change causes you to move in different directions, and growth is simply elevation.

- Be careful not to fool yourself with change and believe it to be growth. You will only greatly grow stagnant; motionless.

- It's possible to have changed in order to satisfy the "idea" of having grown. Or changing from not knowing what exactly to do in order to grow.

"Fear can be a good sign...
It can mean you're at a junction,
and must make a move.
Bt be cautious...
if you don't move
you can be ran over or
simply drift away..."

- Approaching a junction simply means you must go left or you must go right, but factoring in the unknown of what's on the other side can very easily bring about fear.

- Fear isn't always a negative thing. A certain amount of fear can be a healthy sign of progression. Fear only becomes unhealthy, when it's allowed to paralyzes you.

- If you don't act on the fear of a new thing, it will bring you to a complete holt. And just like on a freeway or in a crowded place, if you choose to stop in a place of moving traffic, you will cause a collision, be ran over, or unwilling, you'll drift away with the flow of moving traffic.

- Be conscious of fear, acknowledge it, then act on it.

"Anything you can't explain,
you can't teach...
But you can teach anything
you can explain..."

- Whether it's in life or in a classroom, you know you've learned a lesson when you can explain it to someone else.

- Learning is always by way of a lesson, and or sometimes a series of lessons.

- If you understand it well enough to explain it, you're capable of teaching it.

- If you don't understand what is or what was, "it" will forever be a problem.

- Teaching is simply a balance of solutions between communication and understanding.

"If you don't allow it,

love can't concur much...

When you accept and allow love to live,

it will embrace you, and only then does

it have the power to do what it does...

Concur all things..."

- Love is a choice, and it can only operate under your permission.

- If you're a restricted lover, love will only concur what it can within your restrictions.

- Love only has the power to concur all things when it has no conditions, or restrictions.

- The true experience of love is through forgiveness.

- Vulnerability is the key to being able to love because you must be open to the pitfalls it can sometimes bring.

- No matter what, never be afraid to love again…!

"Don't let your negative thoughts

feed your heart...

Tell those thoughts,

"nah, get up outta here...!""

- Your consistent thoughts becomes a part of consciousness.

- Be aware that what ever you regularly think, will show up in your life one way or another.

- The mind is the strongest muscle in the body, and whatever it produces, it has the power to manipulate the heart, the organs, the entire body…

- It's important to care for your own heart enough to feed it good thoughts.

- Speak directly to negativity. Tell it to go!

"I believe we become overly worried about how people are outwardly LIVING, that we disregard how we are outwardly LOVING..."

- Society has mentally trained us to be judgmental.

- It's possible that we get so caught up in being judgmental of how others are living that we become oblivious and detached of the initial thought of showing love.

- Judging carries a feeling.

"Childish tendencies
has nothing to do with
a child...
But an adult,
mentally or emotionally
damaged and or undeveloped
in particular areas..."

- Childishness can be a reaction of self empathy.

- One may feel sympathy for themselves, and reverting to childlike ways can be a sign of empathic protection.

- It's important to pay attention to what sends you into childlike reactions.

- If you catch yourself in the midst of the act, you can specifically identify the associated feeling and be aware of it in the future.

"If you don't position yourself properly against the wind, it will blow you back. Sometimes you have to lean forward and position yourself to walk against the force."

- Sometimes daily life makes us aware of our situations. We often times get so focused on the small things, that we fail to recognize the force that maybe coming behind a greater situation.

- Stillness can bring a great amount of alertness and understanding. And with understanding, you're able to process a lot of what's going on at hand.

- Being able to make sense of a situation, can bring you to a point of reasoning and sturdy ground to move forward on.

"Good news, bad news...

Accept it because it's all

just a part of the journey.."

- Acceptance should be the first step to all things, but especially if you are moving towards a particular goal(s).

- A journey is simply a traveled path through unknown areas.

- All ups and all downs will be a memory at some point if you don't stop.

- The current road you travel, is your future instruction manual to go further for other journeys.

"Some people never

grasp the art of being themselves."

- Growing into your true self, usually causes you to go against the grain of society as well as the expectation others have of you.

- Peer pressure is so common, we may not always recognize it, but it falls victim to the ways of society.

- Peer pressure has the power to alter a persons true self.

- Art is simply the expression of creativity, and mastering the art of ones self, is to allow the creation of God to flow without allowing the hindrance of society to block it.

- Start questioning yourself. Question your habits. The first steps to learning your true self, is questioning where you are currently. Mind, body, and spirit wise.

"It may hurt and leave you feeling damaged, but all things are good, if only you believe in the way out."

- We're usually quick to believe that when we become damaged, we're no good. But often times it's just the opposite. Without the scars, we know nothing.

- Being damaged is sometimes a part of the process.

- Damages really don't matter if you plan to escape them and believe in your way out.

- The very first step in restoration, is believing you can overcome. Once you believe, the damages slowly but surly reverse themselves and become your testimony.

"Stop stressing...

And make your

struggle your sacrifice...

Lord thank You for the struggle..."

- Whatever is stressing you, give it to God; sacrifice it.

- We don't usually stress over things we don't care about. So if we care enough to stress over it, it is of enough value to sacrifice.

- The technique of letting go, is to completely remove it from your mind. Sometimes you have to specifically replace those thoughts with different thoughts.

"Insecurities are learned and developed through society..."

- Through people around us, society tells us what we should be and what we shouldn't be through media.

- Don't allow society to plant its insecurities in you. It won't allow you to build your own esteem.

- In some cases, insecurities are inherited.

- Insecurities are empty places in the mind that can build into emotional pitfalls of the heart leaving one feeling less than.

- In order to release yourself from insecurities, you have to change your mind and aggressively reverse the insecure thoughts.

"Just like a wound
needs air to aid its healing,
you have to allow yourself to be
vulnerable so it can aid your growth."

- With care, anything exposed has the ability to heal itself.

- An open wound that remains covered in bandages does not heal.

- When we are vulnerable we're often weak yet very conscious. Vulnerability can bring on a new sense of awareness.

- Being open isn't easy because we become aware of the possibility of becoming more damaged.

- In order to open yourself up for healing, you have to first trust yourself. Then in order to seal the healing, you must forgive yourself for believing you were never right or you were never wrong.

"Grow up!
Be superior to
your inferior self..."

- The feeling of being inferior is a mental state.

- Superiority and inferiority is simply the before and after of ones self.

- Self growth shouldn't include the opinions of others. If it does, you'll be in constant conflict between the person you are, and the person you can be.

- We usually associate growing up with becoming mature in responsibilities, but growing up can simply mean growing upward in many other areas as well. Grow up in health, grow up in spirit, grow up in wisdom, ect.

"A leaky roof causes you to search for the leak so it can be sealed.

Pain requires you to search for the problem, if you want to fix it..."

- We're taught not to search out things that disrupt our life. When we come in contact with a deep rooted problem or issue, we usually shy away from it because it unwilling brings buried problems/issues to the surface.

- Sometimes issues from our past, can leak into our everyday life, and we may not even realize it, because we've become so accustom to issues being a part of daily life.

- Pay attention to your patterns. Our past issues often show themselves in continual patterns and habits. Whereas a lot of unhealthy coping habits are subconsciously formed.

"Tears are the escape portal for emotions. Let em out!"

- Tears are purifying.

- We often fail to realize that crying is absolutely normal.

- At some point we have to cry. A build up of compressed emotions can cause insanity. Let them out!

- As healthy as it is to cry, it's also important to know that if you cry 24/7 you'll cry yourself into a flowing river with a current strong enough to take you under.

- Be conscious enough not to cry yourself into self-pity.

- Hold it together and let it out at an appropriate time. Tears are good for your emotional wellbeing.

"A teething baby will cry from pain, discomfort, and possibly a fever, all from new teeth trying to break through tender raw gums.
Let it hurt.... Let it hurt real good....
Once the pain is gone, you'll be equipped to do things you couldn't do before...
Now take a bite into growth...
You've got teeth now..."

- You can't grow into a better place without growing through the pain of what's current.

- Pain is a purging process and it's important to be conscious in your growing, or the pain itself can cause you to renege.

- Pain can be the sign of a birthing process.

"Sometimes you gotta know when to drop your fist and roll with the punches. Doesn't mean you stopped fighting... You just know what's necessary to stay in the fight..."

- A fight isn't always physical, nor does it always involve another being.

- Sometimes a fight comes as a mental, spiritual, or emotional challenge within yourself.

- In order to win a fight it requires you to recognize the challenge at hand, then requires you to be strategic in your approach to overcome it.

- Sometimes in order to win a battle, you have to know when to swing, when to duck, and when to roll. Nothing is learned when one is consistently combative.

"You can't get to the mountain top without the struggle that comes along with the climb..."

- It varies, but the struggle itself is part of the package. Accept it beforehand.

- You can't win without encountering the pressures of struggle. What good is weight lifting without the strain and heaviness of the weights?

- When you view the mountaintop, accept that the process won't be easy.

- When going after anything greater than what you already possess, you will encounter hardships. As long as you constantly remind yourself of the goal, you won't be defeated by hardships.

- If you can't feel the process, it may be too easy. Maybe you should find a more challenging mountain to climb.

"If you don't do what you want to do, what you want to do will haunt you..."

- Regrets often self educed. Forgive and take advantage of life.

- In attempt to satisfy the opinions of those around you, it can causes you veer away from the things you desire as an individual.

- The thought of what you should have, or could have done, can pave a way to your emotions and lead to depression. Choose to live freely.

- Following your desires is often essential to maintaining your sanity.

- When following your desires, it's important to also be rational; be balanced.

"Don't be so cautious
in life that
you miss out on
healthy mistakes..."

- Mistakes are prerequisites to growth, but if you are too cautious of making a mistake, you rarely will.

- Trail and error automatically gives you the opportunity of hands on learning as well as running the process of elimination.

- We're usually taught that mistakes are bad, but what's a trail without and error, and what's a victory without a defeat.

- You've missed the objective of a lesson if you've never made a mistake.

"Working doesn't require worrying..."

- Worrying takes away from your work. It can actually defeat the purpose of working altogether.

- The purpose of working towards a greater thing is to overcome where you currently are. If you're focused on where you're going, it shouldn't worry you on where you are in the moment.

- Worry is a form of fear. It's a fear that is concurred through meditation and relaxation.

- There's no need to worry if you're making progress to be or do better.

- We work in order to eliminate worry.

"If you can't meet your personal challenges face to face, they will intimidate your entire existence."

- Whatever you're afraid of, has power to control your entire life if you don't face it.

- If allowed, fear has the power to become a part of your sub consciousness and you begin to operate in intimidation.

- Fear can be habit forming, when it's used as a shield of defense. Sometimes even used as a defense to guard one from themselves.

- Fear is an emotion. You have to take time to become familiar with the triggers connected to specific emotional fears.

"It may hurt and leave you feeling damaged, but all things are good, if only you believe in the way out."

- As long as you believe in a way out and actually overcome, there is nothing bad thing in anything that assist in positive progression.

- In order to believe for things to be good in difficult situations, you must first accept reality, so you prevent yourself from creating false thoughts.

- Be conscious enough to not become content in negative situations. Being comfortable in bad situations is simply unhealthy coping.

- Always work to change a negative situation to a positive testimony in whatever way you must.

"Don't be afraid
to grow and outgrow
people, places, or things...
Change is extensive.
Only change in areas you feel
is personally necessary."

- Growing and outgrowing is a shedding process. In it's difficulty, be ok with letting go of what you've out grown or what holds you back.

- Change isn't necessarily a part of growth, but it's sometimes necessary for some individuals to begin or continue to grow.

- We all grow at different rates, but if you don't at some point outgrow anything, you'll realize you aren't doing much growing at all…

- If it's necessary, change directions. The need for change can only be determined by the individual.

- Growth is often determined by circumstance, which is why we "outgrow" people, places, and things.

"Sometimes the things that hold you captive are the very things that have the power to set you free..."

- Sometimes the key to development is simply transformation.

- If it's holding you captive, it holds a power that only the individual may know of. That same power it has to hold you down, it has the same power to build you up and out.

- Power is always internal. You are the key to your destiny. So if you allow your natural God given power to hold you down, you can alter that very power and be free.

"To be without your own opinion, is to be without your own mind. Go ahead and disagree sometime."

- It's important to exercise your thoughts.

- Healthy disagreement shows that one is thinking for themselves.

"Often times we ignore our issues b/c they hold us up. Sometimes we need to be held up, in order to move forward."

- Ignoring issues will cause them to become compacted.

- If you don't stop and acknowledge what you've been through, it will hold you up every time you come in contact with something that triggers the issue. It may cause anger, fear, anxiety, or any other personal reaction on the spot.

- It's better to choose to take a pause and blatantly see the issue(s) because it they don't go anywhere, until you acknowledge that they are there.

- Acknowledging and removing the thorn in your side will enable you to move more effectively throughout life.

"If you can be happy with nothing,
you can be happy with anything..."

- Happiness shouldn't require anything, except yourself...

- If you require other things and or people to be happy, you will always find yourself in search of something or someone; always unsatisfied.

- Find the nearest mirror and just stair at yourself. If you feel uncomfortable, you may not be satisfied with you.

- Find a quiet place and write down 5 things you dislike about yourself. Then process why. Make connections. You'll sometimes find that small dislikes are deep rooted issues.

- Keep in mind that being happy with yourself doesn't require anything except love and acceptance of you.

"Without rain, nothing grows, and we go into drought. Stand in the rain and absorb it. You gotta remember what it felt like when the sun finally shines."

- It's important to remember what it all felt like previously, or you'll return to your previous self.

- When in bad times, absorb it all. Since bad times don't last forever, you'll need something to remember in order to keep you out of mental, emotional, or spiritual drought.

- Lifes rainy days, should be your point of reference for after the storm has cleared up, because the season will come again.

"Any GOOD word from a BAD experience, ministers to SOMEONE."

- Keep good words in mind when going through bad situations. Each good word is a weapon.

- Always be willing to encourage someone with your words. They become weapons for them and power for you.

- When sharing a good word with someone from a bad experience, you're letting them know that they are not alone, and you're sharing the warfare of power.

- If your experience caused you to land on a downward spiral, help someone to not land there. They'll remember the exchange of words with you forever.

"If it can break you down,
it can build you up.
In your weakness
stand up!"

- Anything that can be used in one way, can be used in the opposite way. You have to learn how to recycle your break downs.

- If it weighs you down and you learn to push against the force that's weighing you down, eventually you'll be able to tolerate the weight without the stress.

- Whatever the specifics were that broke you down, use those same exact things and reverse your perspective. Change the way you think about the specifics of the breakdown.

- In order to grow strong, you must accept that you will grow weak first.

"If God is in you,
why don't you trust
the God in you...?
You can do ALL things
through Christ Jesus...!"

-   Let that sink in…..

Sabrena S. Henderson

ABOUT THE AUTHOR

I'm just a country girl born and raised in the city. Just like the average person, I've seen good days, I've seen bad days, and I've seen worse days, but my faith in God always kept me afloat whenever I found myself in waters too deep for me to stand in. So all of my writings are faith based because I know Gods glory to be real, and even more prevalent through my way of worship.

Finding myself has been a journey I've been on since high school, and it's been a very challenging, very tedious road, but through all of my nights, I've come to not only see the sun, but I've come to know the Son and I'm willing to die if ever I had to reverse knowing the Son of God.

Without going on and on, let me sum it all up by simply saying I am beyond blessed.

God is good; all the time…!